Hindu
Festival Tales

written by
Kerena Marchant
illustrated by
Rebecca Gryspeerdt

RAINTREE
STECK-VAUGHN
PUBLISHERS

A Harcourt Company

Austin   New York
www.steck-vaughn.com

Festival Tales

Christian Festival Tales • Hindu Festival Tales
Jewish Festival Tales • Muslim Festival Tales

Published by Raintree Steck-Vaughn Publishers,
an imprint of Steck-Vaughn Company

Library of Congress Cataloging-in-Publication Data
Marchant, Kerena.
Hindu festival tales / Kerena Marchant; illustrated by Rebecca Gryspeerdt.
p.   cm.—(Festival tales)
Includes bibliographical references and index.
ISBN 0-7398-2734-0
1. Fasts and feasts—Hinduism—Juvenile literature.
2. Legends, Hindu.
3. Fasts and feasts—India—Juvenile literature.
4. Fasts and feasts—Hinduism—Folklore—Juvenile literature.
[1. Fasts and feasts—Hinduism. 2. Hindus—Folklore. 3. Folklore.]
I. Series.
BL1239.72 .M36   2001
294.5'36—dc21   00-055245

Printed in Italy. Bound in the United States.
1 2 3 4 5 6 7 8 9 0 05 04 03 02 01

Contents

Prahlad and the Demon

Holi is the joyous spring festival. It celebrates new life and the triumph of good over evil. Traditional Holi stories are about one of the most important Hindu gods, called Vishnu. Many Hindus consider Vishnu to be the supreme god (God himself) who, from time to time, comes down to save the world from evil.
At Holi, bonfires are lit to remember events from this story.

A long time ago, the world was ruled by an evil demon. Like all demons, he was the enemy of the gods. He was cruel, and he liked to torture and kill people. Everybody lived in terror of the demon, and they prayed to the gods to save them.

The gods could do nothing to help, because it was impossible to kill the demon. He lived under a spell of protection that said he could not be killed by a god, a human, or an animal. There was no place on land or in the sky, indoors or outdoors that he could be killed. He could not be killed during the day or during the night. He could not be killed by any weapon.

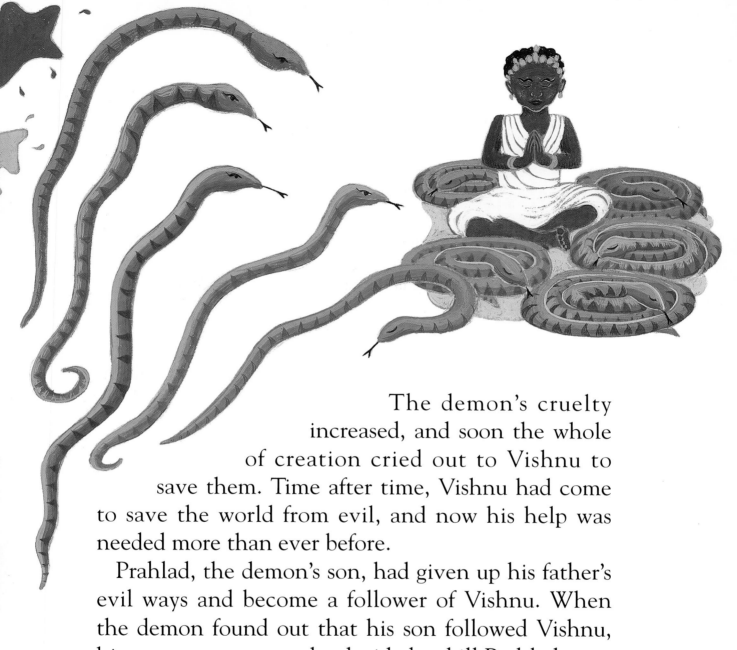

The demon's cruelty
increased, and soon the whole
of creation cried out to Vishnu to
save them. Time after time, Vishnu had come
to save the world from evil, and now his help was
needed more than ever before.

Prahlad, the demon's son, had given up his father's
evil ways and become a follower of Vishnu. When
the demon found out that his son followed Vishnu,
his anger was so great he decided to kill Prahlad.

The demon threw Prahlad into a pit full of snakes.
Some were poisonous and could kill him with a
deadly bite, and some could crush him to death.
Whichever snake killed him, it would be painful!
The demon watched with glee to see Prahlad die.

Prahlad prayed to Vishnu to protect him. The
snakes slept, and Prahlad was unharmed.

Soon the demon lost patience. "He will die!" he cried.

Prahlad was pulled out of the snake pit and tied down on the ground. A herd of elephants were brought to trample over him. The demon watched, expecting to hear every bone in Prahlad's body break. Once again, Prahlad prayed to Vishnu and his prayers were answered. The elephants refused to move.

"Next time you WILL die!" the demon vowed.

A huge bonfire was lit and, as soon as the flames were hot, the demon ordered his sister, Holika, to carry Prahlad into the flames. Holika had magical powers and could not be harmed by the flames, but Prahlad would be burned to death.

Prahlad prayed to Vishnu. As Prahlad and Holika walked into the flames, neither of them appeared to burn. Suddenly, Holika went up in flames. Vishnu had destroyed her magical powers. Prahlad remained under Vishnu's protection and walked out of the bonfire alive.

"Who protects you?" roared the angry demon.

"Vishnu," replied Prahlad.

"Where is he?" screamed the demon. "I will kill him, and he will no longer protect you or anyone from me!"

"Vishnu is everywhere," Prahlad told the demon.

"Is he in that pillar?" the demon mocked.

"Yes," replied Prahlad.

With a deafening roar, the demon drew his sword and charged at the pillar. As his sword hit the pillar, there was a roaring sound, and Vishnu appeared from the pillar in disguise. He had the head and claws of a lion and the body of a man. In this disguise, Vishnu was neither god, nor human or animal, but appeared as half man and half lion.

It was dusk, so it was neither day nor night. Vishnu picked up the demon and carried him to the doorway, so they were neither indoors nor outdoors. Vishnu held the demon, so he was neither on land nor in the sky. Then Vishnu tore the demon apart with his claws, so that he was killed without using a weapon.

Everyone was overjoyed that the demon was dead and his rule of terror had finally ended. Once again, Vishnu had saved the earth from evil, and good had triumphed over evil.

✳ Raksha Bandhan

This is a festival for brothers and sisters. They promise to protect each other, and girls and women give rakhis (protective bracelets) to their brothers, and sweets are exchanged. This poem is from a greeting card that a sister would send her brother.

On this Raksha Bandhan Day
I send you a Rakhi, and firmly pray:
May the glowing Rakhi,
Which adorns your wrist today,
Light your heart with joy and hope
And with love that's strong and true
May it brighten all your days,
Bringing health and strength to you.
God bless you, my dear brother.

Sohan Halva

Sweets are given to everybody as presents during festivals,
and the festival of Raksha Bandhan is no exception.

4 tsp (25 g) cornstarch   12 blanched almonds, cut in half
8 tsp (50 g) sugar   12 cashew nuts, cut in half
1 cup (250 ml) water   12 pistachio nuts, chopped
½ tsp (2.5 ml) food coloring (your favorite color)
½ tsp (2.5 ml) ground green cardamom
3 T ghee (or margarine)

1. Dissolve the cornstarch, sugar, and water in a heavy-bottomed saucepan, and place over medium heat. Stir until the mixture becomes thick and transparent.
2. Add the food coloring, ground green cardamom, ghee, chopped almonds, cashew nuts, and pistachios.
3. Continue to stir the mixture until it comes away from the bottom of the pan. When you can drop some mixture from a spoon and it falls in a lump, it is ready.
4. Remove from the heat, and spread the mixture into a greased baking dish, so it is one inch (2.5 cm) thick.
5. Let the mixture set for 3 to 4 hours. When it has set, cut it into one-inch (2.5-cm) squares.

Warning
Do not cook the sweet mixture without an adult's help.
It will get very hot and could burn you.

Krishna Steals the Butter

The festival of Janmashtami celebrates the birth of Krishna.
This is a story about the time when the god Vishnu
lived on earth as Krishna in order to save the world
from another demon.

When Krishna was born, his uncle, the wicked
demon king, wanted to kill the baby. It had been
foretold that Krishna would kill him one day. To save
Krishna's life, his father smuggled him away to live
in a far-off village among some cowherds. There,
Krishna lived with his foster mother, Yasoda, and
foster father, Nanda. Throughout the god's child-
hood, he was always getting into mischief. His foster
parents, who did not know he was Vishnu, just
thought he was a naughty little boy.

Every day, the women in Krishna's village would milk their cows and use the milk to make butter or yogurt in clay pots. Krishna loved butter. It was his favorite food, and he would do anything to eat it. Every day, he would put his hand in the butter pot and eat some butter, and each day he would eat more and more. Eventually, Yasoda had to hide the butter pots to keep Krishna from eating all the butter. Yet this did not deter the butter thief. Krishna usually found the hidden pots, and, if he didn't, he stole butter from the neighbors' butter pots.

One day, to keep her son from stealing the butter, Yasoda tied the pot of butter to the roof of the house. She thought Krishna was such a small boy he would never reach it. Krishna saw the butter hanging from the roof, out of his reach, and thought of a plan. He asked his foster brother, Balarama, to let him stand on his shoulders. Balarama agreed, and Krishna climbed onto his shoulders. He broke the butter pot with a stone. Krishna and Balarama sat down to eat the butter, but they were soon full and there was plenty of butter left. Krishna then invited his friends, the monkeys, to finish off the butter. Soon, there was nothing left of the butter except broken pieces of the clay pot and greasy finger and paw prints.

12

When Yasoda saw the butter gone and the mess the thieves had made, she was angry. She chased after Krishna, determined to punish him. Krishna thought this was fun and ran around and around. Yasoda ran after him, around the village until, at last, she caught him.

"I'm going to punish you!" she warned. "I'm going to tie you up. That will keep you out of trouble for a little while!"

She brought the rope that she had used to tie the butter pot from the roof and tried to tie it around Krishna. It was not long enough to go around him. Puzzled, she brought another piece of rope and tied it to the first rope, but it still would not go around Krishna. She brought some more rope, but still it would not go around him. Soon she had used all the rope in the house, and still could not get enough to tie up her small child.

13

Eventually, it all became too much for Yasoda. Frustrated and exhausted, she burst into tears.

Krishna felt sorry for her. "It's not your fault that you can't tie me up," he told his mother. "I love you, and I know how much you love me, so I will let you punish me. Go on, tie the rope around me." Yasoda gave it one last try, and the rope easily tied up Krishna, with yards and yards to spare.

Poor Yasoda. She did not know that her child was God Himself, and that no one can tie him up, even with all the rope in the world. Krishna was not actually held by the rope, but by the pure love of his mother.

14

Ganesh Chaturthi

This festival honors the elephant-headed god, Ganesh.
Hindus pray to Ganesh, who is the god of obstacles,
at the beginning of any important event or religious meeting.

Arum, Lord Ganesh,
dressed in white with four arms.
Your color is that of the moon
and your face full of joy.
We worship you so that all obstacles can be removed.

The Ramayana

*Dassehra is a festival that celebrates the triumph of good over evil.
During Dassehra, groups of players and dancers tour India enacting
plays from the epic poem the Ramayana.
These plays are mimes or dances with lavish costumes and masks.
You can perform this play using dance or mime, or a mixture of both.*

Cast of characters

Four narrators

Prince Rama

Sita (Rama's wife)

Lakshmana (Rama's brother)

Hanuman, the monkey general

Monkeys

Ravana, the demon

A golden deer

An army of demons

Props

Bows and arrows for Rama and Lakshmana

Sita's jewelry   A blue sheet, to represent the sea

Orange/yellow/red crepe-paper streamers, for fire

Cardboard swords for monkey army

Masks or face paint for the characters

Indian music for dances/background music (optional)

Cymbals

Narrator 1: Ladies and gentlemen, let me introduce our hero, Prince Rama, banished from his royal palace to live in this forest. Rama is no ordinary prince. He is God himself come to live on earth in human form as Rama.

16

Narrator 2: Rama did not live alone in the forest. His wife, Sita, and brother, Lakshmana, choose to share his exile.

Rama runs on with his bow and arrow, hunting in the forest. Lakshmana runs after Rama, hunting. Sita waves to them.

Narrator 3: Rama, Lakshmana, and Sita were happy living in the forest. Until, one day …

Clash of cymbals. The demon, Ravana, comes on, hiding behind trees and watching Sita.

Narrator 4: The evil demon, Ravana, saw Sita in the forest. He thought she was very beautiful, and he wanted her for one of his many wives.

Clash of cymbals. Ravana waves his hands, casting a spell, and a golden deer comes on. Sita tries to get it to come to her, but it runs off. Rama and Lakshmana see it. Sita points at it, and the two brothers give chase to the deer. Sita is alone on the stage.

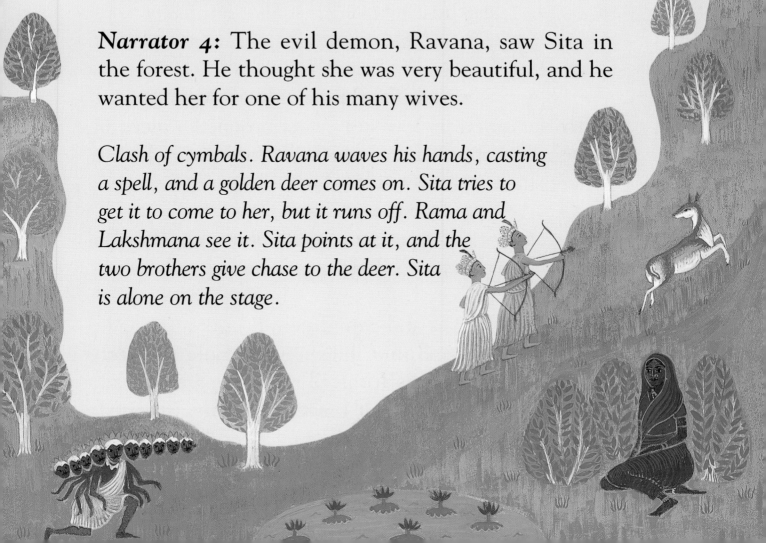

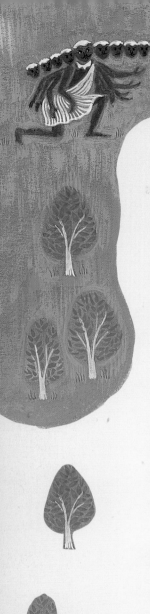

Narrator 1: Ravana cast a spell, and a golden deer appeared. Sita wanted the deer for a pet, and Rama and Lakshmana ran off to catch it for her.

Narrator 2: Sita was alone… at the mercy of Ravana.

Narrator 3: Ravana cast a spell to make Sita follow him. She tried to stay, but the spell was too strong for her, and she had to follow him.

Sita sees the demon. She puts her hands up to resist him and turns her face away. Then, she slowly turns toward the demon and, step by step, approaches him. Ravana beckons her forward, offstage. Every few steps, she drops a piece of jewelry.

Narrator 4: Every few steps, Sita dropped a piece of jewelry so that Rama and Lakshmana could see where she had gone, and find her.

As Sita leaves the stage, Rama and Lakshmana come on from another direction. They are exhausted after a long hunt.

Narrator 1: Rama and Lakshmana couldn't catch the deer and realized that they had been tricked. They returned from their hunt. Then they stopped. Where was Sita?

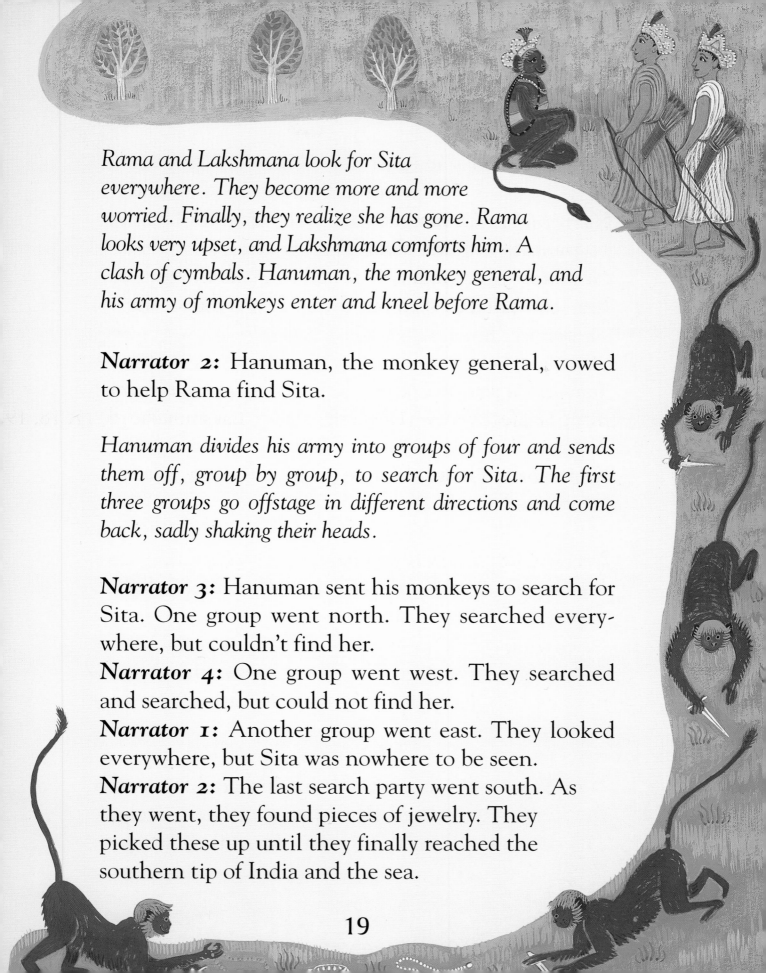

Rama and Lakshmana look for Sita everywhere. They become more and more worried. Finally, they realize she has gone. Rama looks very upset, and Lakshmana comforts him. A clash of cymbals. Hanuman, the monkey general, and his army of monkeys enter and kneel before Rama.

Narrator 2: Hanuman, the monkey general, vowed to help Rama find Sita.

Hanuman divides his army into groups of four and sends them off, group by group, to search for Sita. The first three groups go offstage in different directions and come back, sadly shaking their heads.

Narrator 3: Hanuman sent his monkeys to search for Sita. One group went north. They searched everywhere, but couldn't find her.

Narrator 4: One group went west. They searched and searched, but could not find her.

Narrator 1: Another group went east. They looked everywhere, but Sita was nowhere to be seen.

Narrator 2: The last search party went south. As they went, they found pieces of jewelry. They picked these up until they finally reached the southern tip of India and the sea.

The fourth group goes off in a different direction. Narrators 3 and 4 walk onto the stage with a blue sheet, which they wave on the ground to represent the sea. The search party looks over the water.

Narrator 1: Over the sea lay the island of Lanka, where Ravana lived. Could Sita be there?

The search-party monkeys run back to Rama, carrying the jewelry. Rama recognizes the jewelry as Sita's. The monkeys point to the south. Hanuman kneels before Rama, then sets off in the same direction. All of the other characters leave the stage.

Narrator 2: Hanuman decided to see if Sita was imprisoned on the island of Lanka.

Scene 2: Ravana's palace on the island of Lanka. There are demons guarding the palace. Sita sits alone, looking unhappy.

Narrator 3: Here, in Ravana's palace on the island of Lanka, is Sita.

Narrator 4: Sita hopes that Rama will find her before Ravana forces her to marry him. Shhh! I can hear something!

Hanuman creeps on the stage and slips around the guards. He kneels before Sita. She is very pleased to see him. Suddenly, one of the demons sees them and, after a chase, Hanuman is captured. Ravana walks on to deal with his prisoner.

Narrator 1: Ravana ordered his demons to set fire to Hanuman's tail.

A demon guard sticks the fire streamers to Hanuman's tail. Hanuman jumps in the air and waves his tail around.

Narrator 2: Fire! Fire! Hanuman has set the palace on fire!

Some demons run off and come back with streamers, which they wave in the air. Other demons run off and return with buckets that they use to put out the fire. Hanuman stops, looks at the panic, coolly blows out the fire on his tail, and escapes.

21

Narrator 3: Hanuman returned to Rama. Now that Rama knew that Sita was a prisoner on Lanka, he was determined to rescue her. A huge army gathered to fight the demon army and rescue Sita.

Rama, Lakshmana, and Hanuman lead the monkey army toward Ravana and his demon army. The monkeys have cardboard swords, while the demons wave their arms, casting spells. The monkeys, led by Hanuman, bravely advance toward the demons and touch them with their cardboard swords. To each side of the monkey army, Rama and Lakshmana fight demons with their bows and arrows.

Soon all the demons fall dead, except for Ravana. Rama then moves toward Ravana with his bow and arrow ready. They circle each other. Suddenly, Rama aims his bow and arrow at Ravana's heart. Ravana clutches his chest and falls down dead. Everybody cheers.

Hanuman leads Sita to Rama. Rama and Sita embrace.

Narrator 4: Ravana, the evil demon is dead. Sita is rescued. Good has triumphed over evil!

Hari Krishna

Many Hindu festivals celebrate the god Vishnu's triumphs over evil, especially when he came down to earth in human form as Krishna and Rama. This song is called a bhajan and honors Krishna and Rama. A bhajan is sung by the worshipers singing the words after the leader. Each time the song is sung, it gets faster and faster.

1. Ha - re Krish - na____ Ha - re Krish - na____
2. Ha - re Ra - ma____ Ha - re Ra - ma____

___ Krish-na Krish - na____ Ha-re ha - re.____
___ Ra - ma Ra - ma____ Ha-re ha - re.____

How Sumana Sang for the Goddess Lakshmi

Divali is the festival of lights. It is a time when Hindus hope that the goddess Lakshmi, the wife of Vishnu, will visit their homes and bring good fortune for the next year. The best Divali celebrations take place in the southern Indian province of Andra Pradesh. There, villagers erect platforms and sing songs to welcome the goddess Lakshmi.

In a village in Andra Pradesh, there lived a poor farmer called Deepak and his wife, Sumana. Deepak and Sumana were the poorest people in the village. Their small house was at the edge of the village, where the soil was poor. It was all they could do to grow their vegetables. When Deepak took the vegetables to market, they were always the last to be sold at the cheapest prices because they were so small and ordinary compared to all the others.

Deepak and Sumana loved each other and were happy, despite being so poor. They both wanted a child more than anything else, but, despite their frequent prayers, God did not give them a child. But they were fortunate in one way: Sumana had the most beautiful singing voice in the village and whenever she sang, people would stop their work to listen. During the evenings, the village would gather around a fire to hear her sing.

The festival of Divali was approaching, and everybody in the village was busy getting ready. Because the goddess Lakshmi might visit their homes at Divali, houses had to be cleaned from top to bottom, and clay lamps, called diwas, had to be made. The lamps were so the goddess could see them at night and pay a visit. Many people baked sweets and, outside their houses, drew brightly colored rangoli patterns made of colored rice flour.

25

Deepak watched Sumana clean the house. He was sad because, year after year, they cleaned the house, but the goddess never visited. He wondered if it was because they didn't pray enough or because they were on the edge of the village. Or was it because they were too poor to bake sweets for the goddess and attract her attention with bright rangoli patterns?

Just then, Deepak heard Sumana sing as she went about her cleaning. Even though he heard her sing every day, he was still surprised at the beauty of her voice. Suddenly, he had an idea. He went outside and gathered up some wood that was lying around. He began to make a platform outside the house.

Sumana heard Deepak. When she saw what he was doing, she was horrified. "Don't make a mess," she pleaded. "The goddess will never visit us if the house is untidy."

"Don't worry," Deepak reassured her. "The goddess is going to get such a welcome she will not pass by."

Sumana was puzzled, but she trusted her husband. Why was he making a platform, and why was he making torches to go around the platform?

That night was Divali night, and Sumana and Deepak went without their tiny meal of rice. Instead, they placed their meal on Lakshmi's altar in their house. They said their prayers, and Sumana lit the diwa to guide the goddess to their house.

Deepak then took his wife by the hand and led her outside the house. He lifted her onto the platform and lit the flaming torches around her. "Sing, Sumana?" he asked. "Sing songs of welcome and praise to the goddess Lakshmi. When she hears your voice and learns of our devotion, she will not pass by our house tonight." Sumana stood on the platform and sang into the dark night. Beside her, Deepak prayed to the goddess.

That night, the goddess visited houses all over India. Eventually, she came to Andra Pradesh, and the lights in the houses guided her to Deepak and Sumana's village. Everybody in the village slept, except for Deepak and Sumana. As the goddess came near the village, she heard the most beautiful voice singing songs of praise and devotion to her. The goddess turned toward the sound of the singing and let it guide her toward Deepak and Sumana's house. There she saw Sumana singing on the platform surrounded by torches and saw Deepak praying beside her.

"Why have I never visited this house before?" the goddess wondered. "This couple show such devotion. They have stayed awake all night to welcome me in such a beautiful way." Without being seen, the goddess entered the house to bring good fortune to Deepak and Sumana.

The year that followed was a good year for Deepak and Sumana. Their greatest wish was granted, and Sumana gave birth to a son. Their fortunes also improved when their vegetables grew better and brought higher prices.

The next year at Divali, the couple wanted to thank the goddess for the good fortune she had sent them. Again, they built the platform and Sumana sang throughout the cold, dark night to thank the goddess. The goddess visited them once more to hear Sumana sing.

In the years that followed, all the other villagers built platforms and sang throughout Divali night to welcome the goddess. But nobody sang with more beauty and devotion than Sumana.

Festival Information

There are countless Hindu festivals that honor the different Hindu gods. Festivals can take place at different times all over India and can vary from place to place. The Hindu calendar is a lunar calendar consisting of 12 lunar months. As the months are dependent on the appearance and disappearance of the moon, the dates of the festivals in the Western calendar vary from year to year.

Phalguna

Holi

Magha

Maha Shiva Ratri

NEW YEAR FESTIVALS   These mark the start of the Hindu calendar and are meant to bring good luck. The new year is celebrated in a variety of festivals in different areas of India.

RAMNAVAMI   Falls about a week after new year's day and celebrates the birth of Rama.

RATHA YATRA   The chariot or juggernaut festival that honors Krishna as Jagannatha or "Lord of the Universe." In India, huge chariots decorated with flowers and carvings and carrying a statue of Krishna are pulled through the streets.

RAKSHA BANDHAN   A special festival for brothers and sisters. *Raksha* means "protection," and *bandhan* means "to tie." During the festival, sisters tie a bracelet, called a rakhi, around their brothers' wrists and promise to protect them. In return, brothers promise to protect their sisters. People say prayers and give gifts of sweets.

JANMASHTAMI   Celebrates the birth of Krishna. Pilgrims go to Vrindavan, where Krishna was born. At midnight, the hour of his birth, temple bells ring and a statue of Krishna is put into a beautiful cradle. Pilgrims rock the cradle and pray that Krishna will help them. People tell stories of Krishna; a favorite is the story of how Krishna stole the butter. Groups of boys will enact this story by standing on each other's shoulders to steal pots of milk and rice from high windows.

GANESH CHATURTHI   A festival that honors the elephant-headed god, Ganesh. There are temples of Ganesh all over India, and in every hotel there is a shrine to this god of travelers. This festival is celebrated throughout India.

DASSEHRA   A nine-day festival that celebrates the triumph of good over evil. During Dassehra, groups of actors and dancers tour India performing plays from the epic poem the *Ramayana*, which tells the story of how the god Vishnu came to live on earth as Prince Rama and how Rama killed the demon Ravana who abducted his wife, Sita. These plays are mimes or dances with lavish costumes and masks. Hindu cultural societies are always happy to advise schools who want to put on a performance of the *Ramayana* and may be able to send Indian dancers to a school. Many books on Hinduism have instructions on how to make masks. The festivities of Dassehra fall a month before the festival of Divali.

DIVALI   The festival of light. It is a time when Hindus hope for prosperity in the year to come and hope that the goddess Lakshmi, the wife of Vishnu, will visit their homes and bring them good fortune for the next year. All over the Hindu world, the streets are lined with lights; oil lamps and candles are lit at windows; and outside houses people make brightly colored rangoli patterns on the ground. All of these efforts are to persuade the goddess to visit the home.

MAHA SHIVA RATRI   A festival that celebrates the birth of Shiva, the Lord of Creation.

HOLI   The joyous spring festival. All over India, bonfires are lit, and everybody throws colored paint at each other. This is a festival that celebrates new life and the triumph of good over evil. The traditional Holi stories are about the god Vishnu, who, from time to time, would come down to earth to save the world from evil.

Glossary

Bhajan A song sung by worshipers who repeat the words after a leader.

Cowherds People who take care of cows.

Demon A cruel, evil person or spirit: someone who is against God.

Divali The autumn festival of light.

Diwa A clay lamp that is filled with oil and lit, especially at Divali.

Evil Bad, or harmful.

Exile When a person is sent away from his or her home or country.

Foretold Told of something before it took place.

Ganesh The elephant-headed god who removes obstacles from the paths of religious people.

Glee Delight.

Halva An Indian sweet made from nuts or sesame seeds.

Holi The spring festival.

Incarnation The form of god when he appears in the world.

Krishna An incarnation of the god Vishnu.

Lakshmi The wife of Vishnu. She is the goddess of Fortune.

Lanka The old Indian name for the island of Sri Lanka. The demon Ravana lived in a fortress on Lanka.

Platform A raised, level surface (for example, a train platform).

Pray To talk to God, either silently or out loud, to ask things or to give thanks.

Rakhi A special bracelet given by sisters to their brothers to protect them. The word *raksha* means "protection."

Rama One of the many incarnations of Vishnu, who appeared as an Indian prince.

Ramayana An epic poem about Prince Rama.

Rangoli patterns Patterns of traditional Hindu symbols or flowers drawn with colored rice flour. These patterns are drawn outside houses at Divali.

Spell A saying or some words used as a magical charm.

Torture To make someone suffer lots of pain, as a punishment.

Vishnu One of the most popular Hindu gods. He is the protector of the world and is often considered God Himself.

Weapon A thing—such as a sword, a spear, a knife, or a gun—used to harm someone or something.

Index

Resources

Books

Ganeri, Anita. *What Do We Know About Hinduism?* Peter Bedrick Books, 1996.

Kadodwala, Dilip. *Divali*. Raintree Steck-Vaughn, 1998.

Kadodwala, Dilip. *Holi*. Raintree Steck-Vaughn, 1998.

MacMillan, Dianne M. *Diwali: Hindu Festival of Lights*. Enslow, 1997.

Wood, Angela. *Hindu Mandir*. Gareth Stevens, 2000.

Websites

http://www.hindunet.org
The Hindu Universe: features a Hindu calendar, a glossary of terms and information on Hindu arts, customs, and worship.
http://india.indiagov.org/culture/religion/hinduism.htm
Hinduism: Maintained by the Indian government; gives information on Hindu beliefs and festivals.